FOUNTAIN AND FURNACE

T0345804

Sunken Garden Poetry at Hill-Stead Museum

Sunken Garden Poetry began in 1992 in Farmington, Connecticut, with a single poetry reading in the magical setting of Hill-Stead Museum's Sunken Garden, drawing huge crowds even that first year. Since then the annual series has become one of the premier and best-loved venues for poetry in the country, featuring the top tier of American poets as well as emerging and student writers from the region. From its inception twenty years ago, this poetry festival has given equal weight to the quality of text and the poet's ability to deliver an engaging, powerful, and entertaining experience in the unique theater of the Sunken Garden.

Out of the festival have grown competitions, year-round workshops and events, and educational outreach to Hartford high schools. And while centered at Hill-Stead—with its beautiful views, Colonial Revival house, and priceless collection of Impressionist paintings—Sunken Garden Poetry now engages an ever wider audience through a growing online presence; an online poetry journal, *Theodate* (http://theodate. org); public radio broadcasts; and an annual chapbook prize, now co-published by Tupelo Press.

Sunken Garden Poetry Prize

2014
We Practice for It by Ted Lardner
Selected by Mark Doty

2015
Fountain and Furnace by Hadara Bar-Nadav
Selected by Peter Stitt

HADARA BAR-NADAV

●

FOUNTAIN
AND
FURNACE

TUPELO PRESS
North Adams, Massachusetts

Fountain and Furnace.

Copyright © 2015 Hadara Bar-Nadav. All rights reserved.

Library of Congress Cataloging in Publication Data available on request.
ISBN 978-1-936797-61-5

Cover and text designed by Howard Klein.
Cover photograph: Janet Sternburg, "Phantom." Copyright © 2015 Janet Sternburg
(janetsternburg.com). Used with permission.

First paperback edition: July 2015.

Tupelo Press
P.O. Box 1767, 243 Union Street, Eclipse Mill, Loft 305
North Adams, Massachusetts 01247
Telephone: (413) 664–9611 / editor@tupelopress.org
www.tupelopress.org

Tupelo Press is an award-winning independent literary press that publishes fine
fiction, nonfiction, and poetry in books that are a joy to hold as well as read.
Tupelo Press is a registered 501(c)(3) nonprofit organization, and we rely on
public support to carry out our mission of publishing extraordinary work that
may be outside the realm of large commercial publishers. Financial donations
are welcome and are tax deductible.

For my family, my light

In memory of V.

Contents

Here's a woman's black glove.
It ought to mean something.
　　　　—Charles Simic

I will go on loving as I love the backs
　　　Of things and the invisible . . .
　　　—Lucie Brock-Broido

FOUNTAIN AND FURNACE

Thumb

Who means what it is to be human
and is scarred by childhood.

Thick and neckless. Your head shaped
like a gravestone.

A smile opens across the knuckle and disappears
every time you lift a tumbler of scotch.

Who holds a pen and lies.

Who holds a chopstick
in the language of still-twitching fish.

When you think of the past you form a fist
until a heart beats.

Once removed by a chisel. Then reattached.

You stiffen in the rain and dream
of pudding—a smooth, boneless lake.

Who butters morning toast
while wearing a butter hat.

Who fingers the ad for beef, grows numb
while talking to a girl on the phone.

Useless while typing. Useless
tool who only worships space.

A stump. A blackened stamp.
Your own private map of loneliness.

Who always leans to one side. Detached.
Distant from all others.

FOUNTAIN

Dirty, dirty boy,
what have you done?

Your bath splattered
with cigarette butts, leaves,

the droppings of doves.

No chlorine can clean
your iron-eating years.

Eyes peeled open,
genitals exposed.

A mounting rod lodged
in the base of your back.

Children poke you
and steal your pennies.

The loose change of your mind
emptied by the smallest hands.

Who isn't barbaric anymore?

The people no longer notice
you, bound in stone,

charming
as a taxidermied swan.

Splayed on the plaza square
in mid-spring

you wait to be turned on.

LADDER

Carriage for meat,
the hands and feet

Cascade
of muddied ribs

We keep her
locked in the garage

Or tied up in the back
of a truck

Rust among her many colors

Her shine has gone
nickel-dull

Blond strands
trapped beneath glue

Legs wounded,
strangely delicate, nicked

Heels bound
in black rubber

She steps us closer to God

The farther we are
from heaven, the more we desire

Someone opens her,
someone holds her down

The iron bite of her cry
winds through the streets

We would not touch
the light any other way

WINEGLASS

You swoon inside a cathedral
of cuts and crush the light in your teeth.

Serrated, furnaced, blown to life
by a drunk man who held you with burned hands.

Blisters pearling each of his fingers
that touched the fire of your skin.

The most fragile thing:
                    your waist,
          a single strand of rain.

You take merlot into your overgrown mouth,
tongue your walls, and spit.

Your head perfumed with berry
and French oak.

Grown huge and lidless, your eye
becomes a jellyfish glaring back at you.

You are nightly forgotten
on a nightstand

and once collapsed behind
a typewriter, hoping no one could see.

Flush with lust and panting, you hold
your breath like a child until your belly is filled.

Death to the gypsy fruitfly who dares
to steal your drink.

Blood is your one true wish.

Door

Hung by two pins and swelling,
lacquered and puckering.

Effaced by thumbprints
sealed with grease and ink.

Your quick hands cancel
my gunmetal locks.

No one notices my head, no one soothes
my forehead with a cool cloth.

You handle me, he handles me.

My gold protuberance
available by turns.

I am legless and cannot move.

I am tongueless, mute
to your touch.

I unleash my deranged triangle
of shadows when pushed.

If you look under my skirt you'll see
the darkness of another world.

SPOON

Dimpled by an egg
whose weight vanished

Where a cloud
once rested its head

Cradle of the absent
eye, silver socket

Whose astonishing smoothness
is a torture and an ache

Who services your hunger
but remains nameless

Molten memory curls
along the spine

A furless girl
without arms

She throws back
her hollow head

Flashes the length
of her singular leg

Clutches her thimble
of milk

What is taken
cannot be returned

Her feverish face dissolving
at the bottom of a pool

You reach for her first
thing in the morning

You reach for her
when you cannot sleep

Lulled by her soft
ovals and bells

Telephone Pole

Lightless beacon

who means the death
of green, its useless life.

Is my will to people?

Transmitting
war from house to house.

Chaos rips
through copper,

a haywire noose
tangled around my head.

I once held
the lips of a thousand

sleepy lovers
too far away to meet.

The world become
less strange.

Words for *static*
and *soon*.

Words for *always*
bitten in two.

Years of winter
splintered my throat.

The humming and
the humming.

Your missing
loves return to me

as ghosts with staples
in their mouths.

Drafty wings
on my wires notice me

only as a means
to solicit the sun.

When a man comes
with a drill, I am not

allowed to flinch
but the trembling

hasn't stopped since
I was born.

MOTEL

You are cornflower pale
        and cracked.

Lightly pimpled, you bat
        your occasional eyelash.

You refuse the wind but
        speak of it daily.

Families of gray mice hatch
        and wither inside you.

You stand in the dark for endless
        hours, witness a thousand stories,

let the shadows smear
        your face, and say nothing.

        Watch me leave, return, turn
around, pivot on one foot.

        I enter you, assume the right.

Permanence was a dangerous idea,
        slimsy, blood-lit.

You are my unsteady
        God, subject to brink and collapse.

You hold the hasps and windows,
        house the deepest cuts.

You kneel on the pavement,
        the grass and dog shit.

You displace the outside,
        announce our emptiness.

Nightgown

The seams of me
untethered, plucked.

Slut cut from cotton.

Stained with the milk
of plastic pleasures.

Of lilac and lack,
moth-bitten scrap.

My impossible flowers,
blue hearted.

I worship the silvery
gala of sleep

and the three freckles
below her navel,

then chafe beneath
bed pillows all day

and grow damp, waiting
for her touch.

A threadbare skin
of panting and dusk.

I am the shadow
who contains her

and nightly holds
her freight.

I am her
other I

unreeling,
salt-licked.

BALCONY

Who spends her whole life kneeling
on metal slats and rain.

Ladder for dalliances and thieves.

Of Argentina, of the idea of Argentina,
of never having moved an inch.

Of hanging, being hung, of steel
teeth forked into a brick wall.

Of battery and blistering,
canopy, tarp, and leaking.

Of abandoned nests and spider legs,
the ashen arms of ferns.

Solitary days, touchless nights.

The fire escapes itself,
      the fire never arrives.

Witness of stunted
vistas and hashmarks of light.

Of the dull routine of kitchens
and incessant televisions.

Of a woman dancing in a bra and a man
rubbing the stump of his leg.

Of a tragic daughter put out to dry.

Cage of wrong angles, clanging
her fear of heights.

Of pigeon shit and blueberry foam.

Of petrified lumps of gum that no longer
recall the mouth that spit them.

Of momentary friendships with
          the drift of dead leaves.

Of ten-minute love scenes and briefest
encounters with barefoot strangers.

Ribboned by strands of miniature stars.

The moon illuminates each rusted bar
and cuts her world to pieces.

Of the slow darkness, always
          suspended, always falling.

Of the burden of exile
and snow, the verbless present.

Whipped by the wind of elsewheres.

TRAIN

After Noelle Kocot's "Tu Fu"

Loudly wheels the train
across the table.

Loudly wheels the train.

The pale table,
            its trembling legs.

The night is too knee-scraped
to invite itself inside.

I will not be a cow
in this life, eating

and giving away my ribs
through the barbed wire.

Someone named Ella
eats with me.

She eats with me and does not
know she is dead.

She dines on a bowl
of dried meat.

Sometimes we share an egg.

I never give meaning
to what we say or think of myself

as a tunnel of flesh
that time rips through.

I turn off the lamps
at night. I turn off

the lamps in the day.
I dark. I darken things.

The last line
of every book hurts.

The train rattles me
though it means

I'll never again
be alone, my nightly

visitation
of hooves and ghosts.

OVEN

I live with an oven—
a heavy weight.

I set the timer, skim
its caked corners,

wobble near faint
when considering a square.

Entry. Exit. Door
to nowhere.

Memory framed
by double-paned glass

so I can see the stream
of blue flames caving

the roof of my mouth.

The hiss of history
ablates my face, blisters

my tongue and my name,
numbers me among millions.

I crackle as a leaf.

An entire epoch turned
its face, then washed

its hands for dinner
on an ordinary day.

Who set the table
in silver and lace.

Who opened
the door then closed it.

PAGE

Do not look
up from the one

       tiny mark.

Scare, scar, mar
of it across

       the black irides.

Not even tree,
but its pulped failure.

Space for charting
error's ink-

       dipped slurs.

Sloppy sutures
in milk.

The mind slips,

       shucked loose,

and all the words
for meaning

crushing down,
sheeting the head

      in hospital-white.

I inherited this blighted
alphabet—

      pale palette of ice

crosshatched
by minuses and arrows.

MOUTH

I push my mouth
like a small dog

        away from me.

Mongrel, to whom
do you belong?

On the highway we see hair
stripped from skin,

pimpled, pale
as spoiled milk,

cows packed
into metal crates on I–80.

Their mouths are slack,
anticipating

slaughter, and they will
be slaughtered

in cities like Lincoln
and Des Moines.

My mouth pouts
in the back seat

and weeps, a screwdriver
turning inside my mind.

We are all in pieces
and sad.

We are not Picasso
who could make beauty

       from *a horde of destructions*.

Other trucks drive by,
this time carting

pigs, then horses,
then people.

People stuffed
into crates—

reaching for rain
through the slats.

They did not want
their mouths either,

hungry and crying
and hiccupping black air,

their tireless need
to announce

themselves like
clamorous children

who want and
want, and wail.

CRADLE

There's the ark
in miniature.

There's the vacant
nest in the basement.

Honey-colored limbs,
a fine skeleton, pine.

The elephant and giraffe
plucked out their eyes.

A monkey gutted
himself of clouds.

Turtles fail to circulate,
battery acid caked
beneath their shells.

The stillness and
the stillness.

The pink blanket
in its plastic wrap.

Scent of honeysuckle
and dust.

Let the egg-filled spiders
have their way

and the night cover you.

Saw

Hunger
       was your first word

Born from dust and the whip
       of wrists, you divided
       and divided

Vibrating
       along the line

Sun freckles burned
       into your cheeks

With your unbroken
       jaw and singular need

Devour the limb, the lamb,
       the please

Kiss the hand
       that sold you

Myth and monster,
       machine of teeth

Rain-colored ghost
       whose song is the whir
       and was of aftering

WOOD

The sex of her wild
black knot.

Maple whorl.

Molasses flame
crusting through pores.

Pitted. Weathered.

A brief season
until she hunches

and splits, bored,
bow-legged.

Who will build
a house for her,

a chest for her
hardening heart?

Wrung by years
and rope swings,

inhalation
of the finest papercuts.

She wavers between
burning and blue—

> half buried
> in this earth,

> half in and out
> of hell.

Sentinel who sways
herself to sleep.

FEATHER

Broken machine.

A part abandoned
by its purpose.

The glorious verb
you were.

Torn away, from,
ever.

Your brief home
of air and astonishment

(hushed astronomy).

No clawing after,
no hesitation as you fall.

Misshapen pinwheel
spiked with hair.

Fringes dead and teeming.

Infested shred
of your former self.

The dovecote rejects you.

Without a heart
you do not belong.

The grass flares
its million needles.

Grief crowing overhead.

Who knows the wind
will no longer carry you

or softly set you down.

Who knows every wind
is hard.

Hooklets unhooked,
barbs bent,

vanes that know
no direction.

Your point chewed
off so you can

no longer dream
of drafting

volumes or demand
an audience

for your staggering
descent.

Epic fail, falter, feather,
figment

of cough and thread.

SPINE

Bone ruffle,

hold up the sky
of myself.

Do not abandon

the body
with your precarious

dress of milk and wire.

Threaded hearts,
barbed ornaments.

26 dumb godlets—

their little skulls
bobbing on the line.

Eyeletted, acid-white.

Mere midden,
        such slippage.

Fear in the fiber,

cloud after
cloud on a string.

Hello, unraveling.

Torque of dis-
ease, of wince

and prayer. Stay

with me now, stand
next to the spire

of my crumbling.

SHADOW

Take two Percocet
and dissolve

One is ever haunted

A dark sea, a season
of ghosts

Splashing on the blue wind

The night dragging
behind us

Light, the enemy

       Dark, the enemy

Who will never shine

The other face that shivers
beneath each leaf

Daughter of awnings

She arrives late to dinner
always carting a façade

Drinks all the scotch
in the cabinet

Walks into walls
and grows strange

Diabolical silhouette
with a tusk and a huge head

She inhales entire rooms,
claims every crevice

Straddles the bed
and violates sleep

A black thought

Caught between the eyelid
and the eye

Sun

Blistered apple,
gold that molts

the eye & boils
animals in their caves.

I touch & touch

      & touch,

branding the hands
of each child.

A circle
of unmoored fury.

I see death all
around you—

      your phantomed self
      charred blue,

      cast against
      asphalt.

The body's ash already
visible,

        unglittering
        in its cheap velvet.

Bow down
in the brilliance

        of your borrowed light.

Let me ignite
your end.

HAND

My hand grew big ·
as a house.

It was heavy to carry
and drag through the streets.

I staggered across the lawn
on gravel-burned knees

to watch the home I could
no longer enter.

My wrung wrist turned blue.
My shoulder bled.

Skin tore up my neck
and split open my eye.

> I had given too much.
> I had taken too much.

The hand grew
as the sky grew,

hand the size of wind,

expanding
until it was no longer

my own, until
the weight buried me.

HEART

A bad word
in a poem, smutmouth.

Now wipe the shine
from your lips.

Bordeaux-soaked impulse
murmuring below speech.

You sound like
a limp,

a little ghost
and its echo.

You touch every dead part,
even the toes, farthest
from God.

Hospitals of blood
lie sleepless
in your caverns.

Even tucked inside
the darkness of the body
you will not last.

Quiver of jelly
that collapses a life.

You stole my father
in his sleep.

Flayed fist of twitches
bursting, bound.

Servant with numerous
incisions.

Master
with too many mouths.

A furnace of tongues.

Press your ear
to the wound.

Here the dead sing.

Acknowledgments

Grateful acknowledgment is made to the editors of the following publications in which these poems or versions of these poems first appeared:

Agni: "Fountain" and "Ladder"

Bosque: "Mouth"

Cincinnati Review: "Door," "Motel," and "Spine"

Columbia Poetry Review: "Cradle" and "Spoon"

Crazyhorse: "Thumb"

Green Mountains Review: "Heart," "Nightgown," and "Shadow"

Kettle Blue Review: "Oven" and "Wood"

Meridian: "Wineglass"

The Rumpus: "Telephone Pole"

Sou'wester: "Balcony" and "Feather"

"Thumb" was awarded the 2013 Lynda Hull Memorial Poetry Prize from *Crazyhorse*.

"Hand" was published in *A Glass of Milk to Kiss Goodnight* (Margie/Intuit House).

With many thanks to Peter Stitt for selecting this chapbook for the Sunken Garden Prize, and to Jeffrey Levine and the staff of Tupelo Press. With thanks to kind readers and friends whose vision continues to inspire me: Simone Muench, Kevin Prufer, Wayne Miller, Rebecca Morgan Frank, and Cyrus Console. To my colleagues and students at the University of Missouri–Kansas City. And to Bate and Hudson, always.

OTHER BOOKS FROM TUPELO PRESS

See our complete list at www.tupelopress.org